For You...
Because You're My Friend

The C.R. Gibson Company, Norwalk, Connecticut

What a difference a
friend makes!

THE BEGINNING OF FRIENDSHIP

The beginning of a true and lasting friendship is one of the most important times of life. There really ought to be an "anniversary" or a "birthday of friendship" to commemorate the time when two people became friends.

The trouble is — it's almost impossible for anyone to put a finger on a single day and say, "This is when it all began."

Friendship just doesn't happen overnight. Not the kind that lasts. Its beginning is a long, slow process that can't really be measured by days, weeks, or months.

Oh, you may have met people and thought right away "This is it. We're going to be great friends." Sort of "friendship at first sight."

But this kind of friendship is about as memorable as instant coffee. It's quick, easy and soon forgotten.

Instant friendships often can't last because they are based on only one side of the new person's personality - a sassy smile, a clever remark, an unexpected compliment. You see only the tip of the iceberg and there's so much more to find out about. When you do, you may find that what looked like friendship was only a hope, not a reality.

Now, saying that friendship doesn't begin all at once doesn't mean there aren't any clues that tell a person what may be beginning.

There are plenty of clues.

On first meeting with someone who will

later become a very good friend, there is a feeling...
it's hard to describe but it's kind of an
inner sense that tells you this person is
sympathetic, feeling-like you. That's the
important thing-like you.

And later you find yourself thinking—"What
a neat person, felt as if we'd known each
other before. Wouldn't it be fun if we could do
such-and-such together."

Those clues to friendship remind me of
you and the impression you made on me
when we were first getting to know each other.

When did we first become friends?

You probably can't narrow it down to a
period any smaller than a certain month—
maybe several months. I can't, either.

Something as precious as our friendship couldn't
have been created in just an hour or a day.
It's too big and complex for that. In fact, when

I think of it, it seems that our friendship is still "beginning," because I keep finding out new and interesting things about you all the time.

The beginning of friendship... What a beautiful time. A time that we'll remember, maybe not minute by minute, but by the feelings that have slowly come out of it.

I'm glad that we met and found many reasons to get to know each other better and slowly become friends. Our beginning has been the beginning of so many kinds of happiness for me.

WHAT A DIFFERENCE A FRIEND MAKES

It's true, you know. Having you for my friend has changed so many things in my life. Always

for the better!

When I'm feeling good, being with you makes me feel even better.

When good news comes my way, you're one of the first people I want to share it with.

And on those days when things aren't going so well, just a few minutes with you, even over the phone, can turn the situation right-side-up again for me.

What a difference a friend makes!

And that difference affects so many areas of day-to-day living.

You can go to what promises to be a dull party - with a friend - and have fun!

Cooking can be a routine kind of thing, a chore you'd like to avoid. But when two friends cook together, the work turns into play.

Then when everything's ready and smelling wonderful, a friend is the best seasoning in the world for a really good dinner.

Even cleaning up afterward isn't so bad. Especially if you do it right away so you'll have plenty of time to sit around and talk.

Going places with a friend is always an adventure – whether it's around the world – a Sunday drive in the country – or a "just looking" visit to the shopping center.

A friend even makes a difference in the kind of person you are, the way you feel about yourself.

When you've got a friend you know there must be something going for you. And you want to improve yourself so your friend will like you more than ever.

You do that for me. And so much more. Life is better because of you. You've made a world of difference in my world.

A FRIEND IN NEED IS A FRIEND INDEED
and
WHAT DOES ALL THAT MEAN ANYWAY?

Some of the old sayings have always been difficult for me to figure out.

For instance – "Starve a cold and feed a fever." Or is it – "Feed a cold and starve a fever?" What if you have a cold _and_ a fever?

I may never make any sense out of that one but a saying I think I'm beginning to understand is – "A friend in need is a friend indeed."

Anyone could be confused at first about the meaning of this saying. It sounds like a friend who needs our help is more of a friend because of that need.

Of course, that's not what it means at all.

The real meaning is – the best of friends will always be there to help us if we need help. They are friends indeed.

A "friend when you're in need" kind of friend
is the one who would be perfectly willing to:
  - bring chicken soup when you have the flu
  - water all those demanding plants when
you have to be away.
  - take in some of your visiting relatives
when you run out of beds
  - supply that extra thumb needed to
tie the bows on presents.
  - take care of your cat while you're on
vacation
  - loan you $10 until payday.
  and on and on.
  The point a lot of people miss is that
friends really <u>do</u> want to help out. They may
even be a little hurt if you don't give them
a chance to lend a hand when you need one.
  That's the way I feel about you. Most of all,
I want you to be happy. But if you're unhappy

or troubled for any reason, I want to know about it, to have a chance to help you if I can.

That doesn't mean I want to pry into every area of your life. You and I and everyone have secret places that are meant to be kept private, even when they hurt.

But if you ever felt kind of down or disappointed or confused, I wouldn't want you to ever think it would be too much bother for me if you told me all about it.

At the very least, I could listen. Sometimes that's the best help in the world.

I know you feel the same way about me. Friends would protect each other from all problems or troubles if they could. But if things do go wrong, a friend wants to be told, to be there, doing something to make things right.

A friend in need is a friend indeed. We both know what that means. Hopefully, we'll never get the chance to prove it in a big way, but should that day come, I know you would be a friend indeed. And so would I.

FRIENDSHIP IS A SPECIAL KIND OF LOVE

Remember the movie "Love Story" and what a big success it was? And the book? Millions of people read the book. Millions more saw the movie. Everyone was talking about "Love Story."

Now, I wonder what would happen if someone wrote a book called "Friendship Story"? Would it be a big best seller, with a movie sure to follow?

The chances are that it wouldn't do very well. Friendship just doesn't have the glamour, the excitement, the drama that love does. And yet, friendship is a very special kind of love.

Friendship is a quiet kind of love. It doesn't need a lot of words, repeated declarations of affection to keep it going. Somehow, friends just know when they are together that love is there, too.

Friendship is an undemanding kind of love. It gives freedom to go other places and see other people. Then, when friends get together again, no matter how long they have been apart, they can just take up where they left off.

This freedom is possible because there is no jealousy, no selfishness involved in friendship.

Friendship is a kind of love that never depends on outer beauty. So often, romantic love begins because of physical

attraction. Then, as attractiveness begins to fade, the love may also diminish.

Friendship isn't like that. It is purely a concern for the inner person, a matter of the heart. And, as years go by, the ties of friendship grow stronger and become more precious.

Friendship is an easy-going kind of love. A love that doesn't need soft lights and wine and music. In fact, it's often at its best first thing in the morning when the coffee's brewing and friends are shuffling around in robes and slippers.

It's a love you can depend on- no matter what.

For some reason, it's difficult for friends to talk about the love they feel for each other.

It would be hard for me to simply say,

"I love you," even though I do.

But it's very easy for me to say—"You are my friend and whenever I think of you it is always—with love."

FRIENDS ARE LIKE MIRRORS

There are mirrors and then there are mirrors.

Anyone knows this who has ever looked in a mirror in a room where the light is very soft and indirect. That kind of a mirror can tell you wonderful things about your face, even though they may not be true.

The mirrors in the produce case at the supermarket will tell you quite a different story.

Fun house mirrors at a carnival can

make skinny people fat and vice versa.

One-way mirrors can be deceiving or re-
vealing, depending upon which side of
them you are standing.

Friends are like mirrors because friends
let us look at ourselves. But friends are
better than mirrors because no matter
what the light or angle happens to be, the
reflection we see in the face of a friend is
always true.

Because you are my friend, you are like
a mirror to me. A very special mirror that lets
me see myself as I really am.

Your face is my most reliable mirror
and if I sometimes see expressions there
that I don't want to see, that just tells
me it's time to make some changes in my
life.

If I'm coming across a little affected,

even phony, I can see it in your face. You would never say – "Now, stop that!" – but you don't need to. Just a look at you and I know.

Sometimes I try to appear cheerful and bright when I'm feeling cheerless and depressed. Your face tells me that my act isn't very convincing. And that's good, because then I can just drop the pretense, talk things out frankly and start to feel better right away – really better.

When I'm at my best, feeling full of joy, the reflection of me I see in your face makes me even happier.

You're a perfect mirror of all of my moods. And the best thing is that you are a caring mirror, sharing, feeling, understanding – never cruel or judgmental.

When I see myself reflected in your eyes,

I can see clearly all the possibilities for improvement and goodness within me. And no other mirror in the world could ever allow me to experience myself so deeply and fully as you always do.

Thank you for those silent truths that reflect the way I really am — on the outside and the inside, too.

THE E.S.P. OF FRIENDSHIP

People talk a lot these days about extra-sensory perception, the ability to receive thoughts without words. No one knows for sure if this kind of communication really exists.

But I think it does because I have experienced the ESP of friendship with you.

There have been so many times when I have been thinking of you, wanting to talk to you. Then the phone rings and I know, even before I hear your voice, that it's you.

There have been so many occasions when, out of the blue, we have both said exactly the same thing. We laugh about these "coincidences" but I wonder if they aren't evidence of a communication that goes beyond speech and hearing.

Of course, the fact that we have known each other for a long time has sharpened our ability to read each other's thoughts. But I don't think that it can all be chalked up to familiarity. I simply feel more in touch with what you're thinking than I do with others. And when we're together at some gathering and I want to tell you —

"Look at the size of that diamond," or "The onion dip tastes kind of strange,"—all I have to do is give you a meaningful look, and you know.

It makes me think that we are more than two strangers brought together by chance. This mysterious communication that we share seems to be evidence that we are truly related in a way that goes beyond blood, that we are kindred spirits, one in heart.

IT WAS THE WORST OF TIMES:

IT WAS THE BEST OF TIMES

Friendship has been described as having the mathematical power to divide unhappiness and multiply joy. I know this is true because friendship, especially your friendship, has done this for me.

This ability to change a mood and alter an outlook doesn't come about from any mystical hocus-pocus. Friends can turn the worst of times into the best of times simply by sharing. Of course sharing can only come out of a lot of caring but friends do care, no matter what kind of time it is. They care enough to be there, live and in person, when everyone else has made some feeble excuse and gone on to greener pastures.

Take the experience of moving. Now, no one likes to move, even if it's only from one part of town to another. Just the thought of all the packing, lifting, sorting, discarding and cleaning up can put a person in a pretty grim frame of mind before the actual move takes place.

Only the people who really care about you would volunteer to share such an experience. Only a real friend would pitch right in, early on moving-day morning, to take part in the "terrible transfer."

But not only will a friend help, a friend will help eagerly and happily. And all of a sudden what could have been a bad time turns out to be a good time!

When a friend shares an experience like moving day, it can actually be fun. The small tragedies of broken dishes and scratched furniture end up making you laugh instead of cry. And when the job is finished and you're sitting around in your new place, surrounded by packing crates, drinking coffee, you can look back on it as not so bad after all, really pretty invigorating.

It's the sharing that makes all the difference.

And it gives you a pretty good feeling when a friend really wants to share a situation that you don't even want to be in yourself.

A friend can make the worst of times the best of times. And, of course, when some especially glad occasion comes along, a friend can make the best of times better than ever!

PEOPLE ARE BETTER

Is the dog man's best friend? I don't think so. People are better.

Are diamonds a girl's best friend? Perhaps for a "girl," but a mature, feeling person would probably find them somewhat lacking in warmth and understanding. People are better.

We've heard a lot about being "friends with our houseplants." It's easy to like plants and be proud of their growth and beauty. But when it comes to friendship, people are better.

I like dogs, diamonds and dahlias very well. But when it comes to friends, people are better. Especially wonderful, giving, caring, loving people... like you.

FRIENDSHIP — NOT FOR SALE

There are people who try to buy friendship — or what passes for friendship, maybe companionship, "security" — so they acquire cocker spaniels or pear-shaped pendants or potted palms.

There are pet shops, jewelry stores and plant shops in every shopping center. But there isn't any store in the world where you can go and buy a friend.

If there were such things as "Friendship Stores" probably everyone who could possibly afford it would have a friend.

But friendship is not for sale.

That's not to say that friendship is free, yours for the asking. We all have to pay a price for friendship that goes beyond money.

Friendship requires choice, risk, honesty, patience, time, and ultimate concern.

First of all, we have to choose our friends and this should be given a good deal of thought, since a friendship wisely chosen can last for a lifetime.

Then comes risk. Some people are afraid to take the risk of offering themselves to another person. They are afraid of rejection. And rejection may come. But unless you put out your hand and offer yourself, friendship can never become a reality.

Friendship requires honesty and this is also a difficult price to pay. We are so used to wearing masks, hiding our real selves from the world. But unless you are really "you" with another person, true friendship is impossible.

It takes a lot of patience, a lot of time to form a lasting friendship. And more of both to keep it going strong. Some people are just "too busy" to give that much of themselves.

Most important, friendship requires an

ultimate concern, a desire to do everything
in your power to keep your friend happy and
your friendship alive.

Spelling out all these "prices" that have to
be paid for friendship makes them seem kind
of overwhelming. But, you know, when you like
someone a lot it's not so much a payment
as it is a gift. And for every gift you give a
friend, so many more are given in return. Friend-
ship is a real bargain!

REMEMBER THE LAUGHTER

When I look back on our friendship, there
are so many memories of times we've spent
together. I'm grateful for every one of them,
but my favorite memories are of the times
when we've simply laughed, had fun, and

enjoyed ourselves.

Laughter is a funny thing, not just funny ha-ha, but funny strange, because what strikes one person as laughable may strike another as silly or weird or pointless.

But we usually agree on what's funny. Maybe we have matching funny bones. Anyway, I know that when something really breaks you up and you laugh till you cry, almost always it strikes me the same way.

Remember the laughter we've shared. There's been so much of it we could never remember it all.

But whenever I look through old snapshots of us, I do remember those happy, laughing times. Some of them are still good for a laugh—the now strange hair styles, the clothes that were pretty funny even when they were

in fashion.

I see pictures taken on trips we took to places we couldn't wait to get away from—but they were fun anyway.

And there are all those shots taken at parties with us together and others standing nearby, looking like they are thinking "Those two are the silliest ever."

The pictures I like best are the ones of the funny times that are kind of inside jokes with us. Show them to anyone else and not a smile would be cracked. But just one look at them and I'm laughing all over again.

It makes me smile and feel very glad just knowing that I'll always have a lot of laughter to remember because I'm lucky enough to be friends with an unforgettable _character_ like you.

THE QUIET HOURS

Friendship is a talkative relationship
and when good friends get together, the
talk always flows easily and spontaneously.
Friends never have to think about what they're
going to say to each other. And they never
have to measure their words carefully to
avoid any sensitive areas. Good friends can
say just about anything to each other, knowing
that their confidences will be kept and
if any slips-of-the-tongue are made, they
will be forgiven and soon forgotten.

Friends really make conversation an art
because they are just as interested in listen-
ing as they are in talking. So the ideas go
back and forth, the subject changes abruptly
and often, and the time goes by much
too swiftly.

Friends who can talk so freely and easily to each other can also do the opposite. They can be together without saying a word and never feel in the least uncomfortable.

The ability to be silent with another person may sound like one of the simplest things in the world. But it's really something rare and precious that only two people who know each other very well can share.

With a new acquaintance, silence is something we try to avoid. It seems almost rude to let the conversation lag and if it does both people will search frantically for something to say just to fill up the uncomfortable and embarassing gap.

But with a friend, the quiet hours can be more pleasant to share than any others.

It's good to remember times spent with

you when we've said very little because, at those particular times, words weren't needed.

Think of the times when we've watched some special TV show or when we've gone to the movies together. And maybe we haven't said a word for an hour or more. But we didn't need words because we both knew how much the other was enjoying the unfolding story.

Driving together through the countryside on a crisp autumn day, we can go for miles and miles without speaking, just drinking in all the beauty around us and sharing the silence.

Then there have been times when we have been together in the evening, reading perhaps, or just looking at the firelight, and without talking we have shared a very special communication that not everyone gets to experience.

It is the knowledge that we can be together without talking and know a warm feeling of ease and togetherness that words would spoil somehow.

Those are the times when it seems that we communicate with each other best of all. And those quiet hours make me think how true the old saying is — "Speech is silver but silence (especially silence shared with a friend) is truly golden."

LONG DISTANCE FRIENDSHIP

In the beginning of friendship, it is important that new friends get together often. During that "getting to know you" time, each needs to see each other, face-to-face, so their new friendship can grow strong and lasting.

And, of course, friends want to be near each other always. But life has a way of separating people - sometimes just for a few weeks and sometimes for much longer.

But once friends become really close, in mind and heart, then their friendship will live on no matter how far apart they may be, no matter how long they go without meeting.

When I've been far away from you, thoughts of you seem especially vivid in my mind. And often just when I'm thinking of you and missing you the most, the phone will ring bringing your voice and all the news from wherever you may be.

Those are the times when I'm especially anxious for the mailman to arrive. When he brings me a letter from you, I feel almost as close to you as if you were here with me.

Closer in one respect, because I have proof,
in writing, that you were thinking of me, too,
and that you took the time to sit down and
share a few minutes with me, friend to friend.

When you're away, I sometimes get the
feeling that you really are a "second self,"
that while I'm here another part of me is
far away, having new experiences and seeing
new things that will soon come back to me to
enrich my life.

Best of all, I like it when we're near to
each other so we can go places and do things
together. But when we're apart, even though I
miss you, I feel that a part of me is there
with you and a part of you is here with me.

And I know that when we see each other
again, nothing will be changed, and we
can pick up our friendship, easily and eagerly,
right where we left off.

GIFTS WITHOUT RIBBONS

Friends give each other so many gifts
through the years. And not just on special
occasions. There are all those times when
you pass a shop window and see some-
thing and think — "That just looks like my
friend. I'll buy it as a little surprise!"
Usually these gifts aren't large or expen-
sive, but the smallest present, when it
comes from a friend, brings a very special
kind of happiness.
There are other gifts, too. Gifts without
ribbons. And friends have a way of exchanging
these almost every time they meet. They
don't cost a thing, but very often they are
prized more than anything you can hang
in a closet or put in a drawer.
Gifts without ribbons are the expressions

of kindness and love, which friends store in their memories and treasure in their hearts.

Of all the gifts you've given me, the gifts without ribbons are the ones I appreciate most...

The times when you've listened so carefully when I've really needed to talk and sort out my thoughts. The advice you've given me that has helped me find good and useful parts of myself I didn't know were there. These are gifts without ribbons.

Your encouragement just when I've needed it so much. Your praise for things I have worked hard to accomplish. Your genuine happiness when something wonderful has happened to me. Gifts like these don't need any fancy wrapping.

The secrets you have shared with me and

the secret parts of me that you always keep safe and secure. The way you sense my changing moods and respond to however I may be feeling. Your smile that makes me smile along with you. Just knowing you're my friend. These are all gifts without ribbons that you have given me.

You'll never know how much they've always meant, how much they mean today. Thank you for giving me those parts of yourself which bring so much happiness to me.

TIFFS, SPATS, SQUABBLES AND OTHER BRIEF UNPLEASANTRIES

You and I are so much alike in so many ways. I don't think I've ever known anyone who was so much like me.

Still, we have our differences as all friends

do. And that's as it should be. Think how boring our friendship would be if we both agreed on absolutely everything. If we were exactly alike, neither of us could ever bring anything new to the other. Talking would be a waste of time since we would always know ahead of time just what the other was going to say.

It is precisely our differences that keep our friendship interesting and help us both to learn and grow.

But these differences do cause some stormy situations from time to time. Nothing big and ugly. No shouting matches or out-and-out knock-down-and-drag-out fights.

You and me? Really fighting? That's really kind of funny even trying to imagine.

But once in a while, we have our little tiffs, our minor misunderstandings. They only last for a few minutes and then we may be a little cool with each other for a day or so. But then you call me or I call you, we make up, maybe laugh about how silly we've been, and forget the whole thing.

Those brief unpleasantries that come up now and then are healthy in a way. They prove that we're not afraid to speak our minds to each other. They show that we both know that our friendship is strong enough to survive these sudden, unexpected spats.

Afterwards, we may both feel the same as we did before about whatever caused it all. But the important thing is we have disagreed and then we have agreed to dis- agree and go on from there.

Voicing those disagreements helps us to build understanding and our friendship is stronger for it.

There's nothing wishy-washy about our friendship. I'm me and you're you and on a few subjects, never the twain shall meet. But knowing that, we respect each other all the more.

By saying what we really think to each other, we really communicate. And who knows, maybe some day I may even bring you around to my way of thinking on a thing or two. At any rate, it's fun trying.

BECAUSE YOU'RE MY FRIEND

Because you're my friend . . .
That's a sentence that has so many different endings, all of them positive and meaningful.

Because you're my friend, I have a good feeling about myself, since you have chosen me to share an important part of your life.

Because you're my friend I've known so many more "peak experiences". You have multiplied all my joys and divided my feelings of unhappiness.

If I ever need any kind of help or advice or encouragement, if I ever need someone just to be there, to listen, I know I can count on you ... because you're my friend.

Because you're my friend, I've known that special, free and easy kind of love that only two friends can share.

I've been able to look in your eyes and see myself as I really am.

I've learned a new kind of communication, the ESP of friendship, that goes beyond speech and hearing, that is more a matter of the heart.

Because you're my friend, even the moments that I've dreaded, thinking they would be the worst of times, turned out to be the best of times thanks to you just being there with me.

And you have shown me the true value of friendship, that wonderful human commodity that isn't for sale in any store in the world.

Because you're my friend I have such a wealth of memories, some of parties, fun and laughter... some of quiet hours when we really didn't need any words.

Because you're my friend I know that there will always be at least one person in the world who will be close to me, whether near or far apart.

Because you're my friend I have found the freedom to truly be myself, to be completely honest even if it means we have to disagree and then agree to disagree.

And so much more. I could never tell you what a difference you have made in my life.

But I want you to know that you're a very special person in my eyes and that when I think of you it will always be "with love"... because you're my friend.

PHOTO CREDITS

Elizabeth P. Welsh—Cover; Pat Powers—p.2; Four By Five, Inc.—p.7, p.10, p.30; Penny Pederson—p.15; Michael Powers—p.19; Bruce Ando—p.23, p.38, p.55; Ray Mainwaring—p.35; Jacqueline Marsall—p.42; Don Davenport—p.47; Stanford Burns—p.51; Gene Ruestmann—p.58.

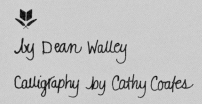

by Dean Walley

Calligraphy by Cathy Coates